ANIMALS ON THE EDGE

Polar Bears' SEARCH for ICE

A Cause and Effect Investigation

by Gillia M. Olson

Consultant:
Steven C. Amstrup, PhD
Senior Polar Bear Scientist
USGS Alaska Science Center
Anchorage, Alaska

CAPSTONE PRESS
a capstone imprint

Fact Finders are published by Capstone Press,
151 Good Counsel Drive, P.O. Box 669, Mankato, Minnesota 56002.
www.capstonepub.com

Books published by Capstone Press are manufactured with paper
containing at least 10 percent post-consumer waste.

Library of Congress Cataloging-in-Publication Data
Olson, Gillia M.
  Polar bears' search for ice : a cause and effect investigation / by Gillia M. Olson.
    p. cm. — (Fact finders. Animals on the edge)
  Summary: "Describes polar bears and their disappearing habitat"—Provided by publisher.
  ISBN 978-1-4296-4532-4 (library binding.)
 1. Polar bear—Juvenile literature. 2. Polar bear—Effect of global warming on—Juvenile literature.
I. Title.
  QL737.C27O38 2011
  599.786'17—dc22
                                                          2010007719

Editorial Credits
Marissa Bolte, editor; Ashlee Suker, designer; Kelly Garvin, media researcher;
    Eric Manske, production specialist

Photo Credits
Alamy/Steven J. Kazlowski, 26
AP Images/Marco Garcia, 24
Dreamstime/Gail Johnson, 6; Gmvozd, 23; Laura Jelen Kovich, 14; Outdoorsman, 5, 8;
    Paul Van Slooten, 27; Vladimir Seliverstov, cover, 9
Minden Pictures/Flip Nicklin, 22
Nature Picture Library/Andy Rouse, 16; Steven Kazlowski, 11
Peter Arnold/Ingrid Visser, 4
Seapics/Bryan & Cherry Alexander, 18, 20
Shutterstock/Florida Stock, 10; Gardawind, 17; Morozova Oxana, design element (ice);
    Robert HM Voors, 21; Thomas Barrat, 15; Tonylady, 19

TABLE OF CONTENTS

CHAPTER 1 | What's Happening to Polar Bears? 4

CHAPTER 2 | No Frozen Dinners 12

CHAPTER 3 | The Meltdown 16

CHAPTER 4 | Solutions 22

Reduce Your Carbon Footprint 28

Resources to Help Polar Bears 29

Glossary 30

Read More 31

Internet Sites 31

Index 32

What's Happening to Polar Bears?

News programs report the plight of the polar bears. Commercials for wildlife groups show pictures of cute polar bear cubs floating on melting chunks of ice. The sad music that plays in the background tugs at your heartstrings. You might be wondering what's happening.

On May 14, 2008, polar bears were listed as "threatened" under the **Endangered Species Act** of the United States. Threatened species are not quite in danger of dying out, but they soon could be.

Polar bears are found in the United States, Canada, Greenland, Norway, and Russia.

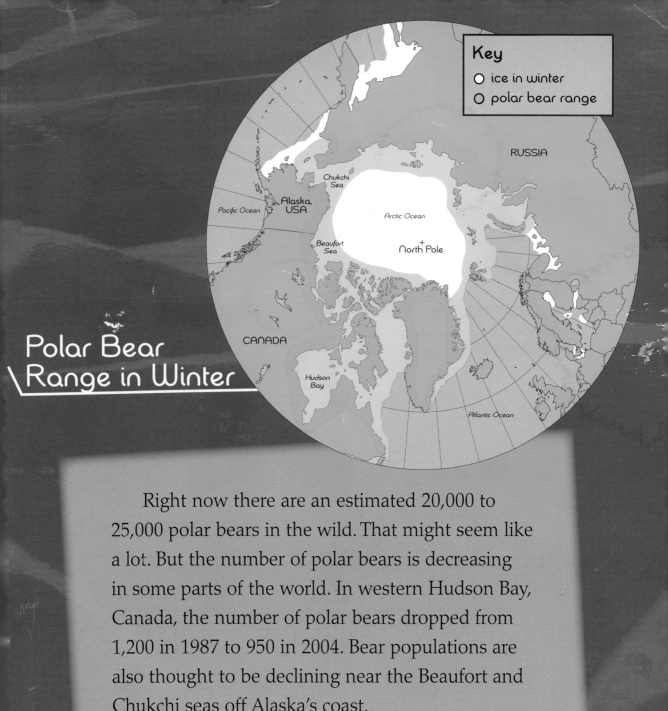

Polar Bear Range in Winter

Key
- ○ ice in winter
- ○ polar bear range

RUSSIA

Chukchi Sea

Alaska, USA

Pacific Ocean

Arctic Ocean

Beaufort Sea

+ North Pole

CANADA

Hudson Bay

Iceland

Atlantic Ocean

Right now there are an estimated 20,000 to 25,000 polar bears in the wild. That might seem like a lot. But the number of polar bears is decreasing in some parts of the world. In western Hudson Bay, Canada, the number of polar bears dropped from 1,200 in 1987 to 950 in 2004. Bear populations are also thought to be declining near the Beaufort and Chukchi seas off Alaska's coast.

Endangered Species Act—a U.S. law designed to protect plant and animal species in danger of dying out, or endangered

Polar bears eat small whales, birds, reindeer, and even eggs and sea plants when food is scarce.

Polar bear populations are showing other problems too. Scientists are noticing that adult bears weigh less than they used to. And fewer cubs are surviving their first year of life. These signs point to the fact that polar bears may be facing **starvation**.

Researchers have found several examples of male polar bears stalking females and young adult bears. Even when food is easy to find, male bears are known to kill cubs. Less often, a fight over mating may result in one bear being killed and then eaten. But what scientists have seen recently is different.

starvation—suffering or dying from lack of food

Scientists saw clear evidence of large bears stalking, killing, and eating other smaller adult polar bears. These behaviors are seen only when polar bears are having a difficult time finding food.

The bears' search for food has brought them into more contact with people. Over the last 40 years, attacks on people, homes, and campsites have tripled in the western Hudson Bay area. And the increased attacks come even as the polar bear population has gone down.

Polar Bear Basics

Scientific Name: *Ursus maritimus*

Weight: Males: 900 to 1,600 pounds
(408 to 726 kilograms)
Females: 300 to 800+ pounds
(136 to 363 kg)

Length: Males: up to 10 feet (3 meters)
Females: up to 8 feet (2.4 m)

Life Span: 20 to 30 years old

Reproduction: Females have first young at 4–8 years old
Only average five litters of cubs in a lifetime

Young: One to three cubs; twins are most common
Size of guinea pig at birth
Live with their mother two to three years

To understand why polar bears may be starving, we need to know how they live and hunt. Polar bears spend the long Arctic winter and early spring hunting on huge sheets of sea ice.

Ringed seals are the polar bears' most common prey. Seals raise their pups in snow dens on the sea ice. Bears raid these dens for easy prey. Seals also use holes in the ice to breathe between dives. Polar bears wait by these breathing holes and pounce when the seals come up for air.

Polar bears can find a seal's breathing hole under nearly 3 feet (91 centimeters) of ice and snow.

Big claws and paws help polar bears grab seals that weigh 150 to 200 pounds (68 to 91 kg).

Because polar bears are huge, they need to eat a lot. Seals are a very fatty food. A fully grown polar bear needs an average of 4.4 pounds (2 kg) of seal meat a day to survive. When seals are plentiful, polar bears may eat only the fat off a seal kill. Then they move on to the next prey.

The bears also eat a lot to build up fat for seasons when food is harder to find. In southern areas, polar bears spend the entire summer on land. There are no seals to catch on land. The bears must wait for the ice to refreeze in fall. They might try to find a few scraps of food, but mostly they live off their fat stores.

Polar Bear Adaptations

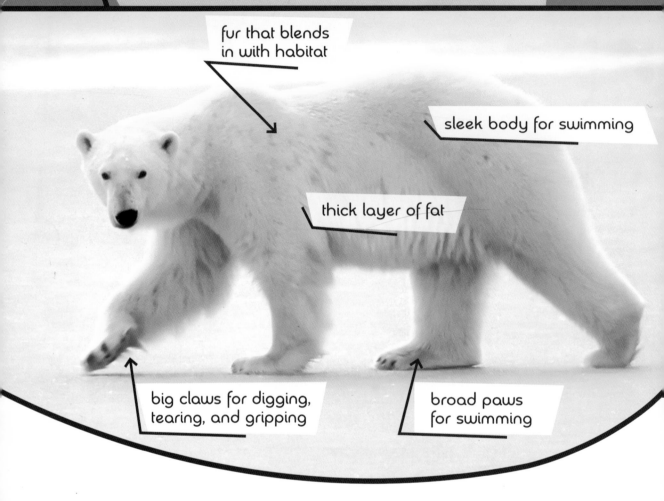

fur that blends
in with habitat

sleek body for swimming

thick layer of fat

big claws for digging,
tearing, and gripping

broad paws
for swimming

Bears are well-adapted to their harsh polar environment. Winter temperatures in the Arctic can plunge to minus 50 degrees Fahrenheit (minus 46 degrees Celsius). Despite the cold temps, polar bears maintain a body temperature about the same as humans—96.6°F (36°C).

Polar bears swim at speeds of about 6 miles (10 kilometers) per hour.

Polar bears are strong swimmers. They often paddle as far as 15 miles (24 kilometers) while traveling to new sea ice. Polar bears have been seen swimming hundreds of miles in calm waters to find new hunting grounds.

In 2004 researchers found four drowned polar bears after an Arctic storm. No one had reported seeing drowned bears before. Polar bears swim well in calm waters. But in this case, waters were rough and stormy. The pack ice was also 160 miles (257 km) away. Some bears simply couldn't handle the rough water combined with the long distance. They were searching for ice, but they couldn't get to it.

WHAT IS HAPPENING TO THE SEA ICE?

CHAPTER 2
No Frozen Dinners

Each year the huge sheet of ice on the Arctic Ocean goes through a cycle of freezing and thawing. The ice sheet is biggest in March and smallest in September, at the end of summer. The cycle is normal, but temperatures in the Arctic are on the rise. The higher temperatures are causing more ice melt than usual. From 2002 to 2009, the summer sea ice has been between 15 and 39 percent below average.

Decreasing summer ice makes hunting difficult for polar bears.

Higher temperatures also mean the ice melts earlier in spring and freezes later in fall. Animals in the southern parts of the polar bear range feel these effects the most. There, ice melts entirely in summer. In recent years it has been melting earlier and freezing later. Higher temps have added at least three weeks to polar bears' time off the ice. On land, the bears can lose as much as 2.2 pounds (1 kg) of body weight each day.

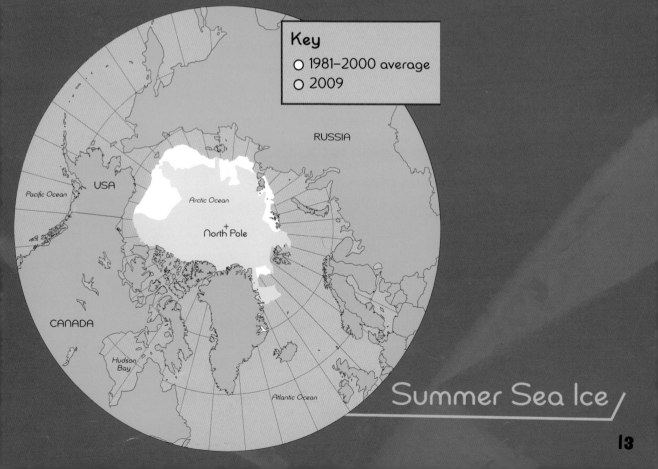

Key
○ 1981–2000 average
○ 2009

RUSSIA

USA

Pacific Ocean

Arctic Ocean

+
North Pole

CANADA

Hudson Bay

Atlantic Ocean

Summer Sea Ice

Polar bears are built to stay warm. But this means they overheat easily, especially away from the ice.

Why can't polar bears just start hunting prey on land? The biggest reason is their size. Males weigh more than 1,000 pounds (454 kg). They need their rich diet of marine mammals to keep their large bodies healthy.

To compare, brown bears in the Arctic rarely reach weights above 440 pounds (200 kg). Smaller brown bears can get by with plants, fruit, and the occasional fish. Large polar bears require more calories than this diet could offer.

Polar bears have developed over 250,000 years to hunt seals. They cannot reverse that behavior overnight. Even if they could, they would be competing with brown bears that have evolved to hunt on land. In nature, the animals best suited to their environment win. If brown bears have already adapted to life on land, how could polar bears compete? Polar bears are made to live in Arctic conditions. Outside those conditions, they are at a great disadvantage. They need that ice.

WHAT'S CAUSING THE ICE TO MELT?

CHAPTER 3

The Meltdown

The sea ice is melting because the world is getting warmer. Average global temperatures have increased 1.37°F since the 1800s. How could a rise of less than 2 degrees be such a big deal? Consider the difference between 32°F (0°C) and 33°F (0.6°C). At 32°F, water freezes. At 33°F, it doesn't. Polar areas have seen the biggest change. In parts of the Arctic, temperatures have risen at more than double the global rate.

Polar bears were the first animals to be listed as a threatened species because of global warming.

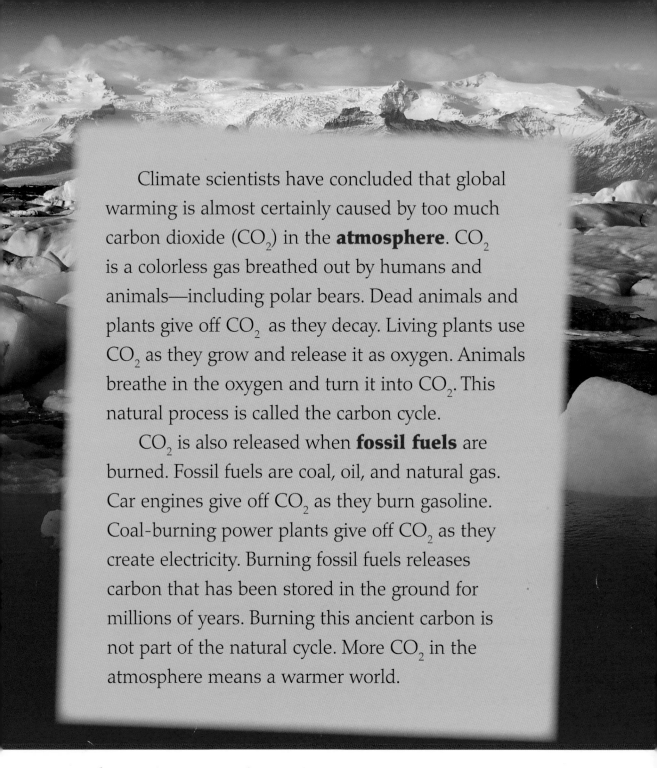

Climate scientists have concluded that global warming is almost certainly caused by too much carbon dioxide (CO_2) in the **atmosphere**. CO_2 is a colorless gas breathed out by humans and animals—including polar bears. Dead animals and plants give off CO_2 as they decay. Living plants use CO_2 as they grow and release it as oxygen. Animals breathe in the oxygen and turn it into CO_2. This natural process is called the carbon cycle.

CO_2 is also released when **fossil fuels** are burned. Fossil fuels are coal, oil, and natural gas. Car engines give off CO_2 as they burn gasoline. Coal-burning power plants give off CO_2 as they create electricity. Burning fossil fuels releases carbon that has been stored in the ground for millions of years. Burning this ancient carbon is not part of the natural cycle. More CO_2 in the atmosphere means a warmer world.

atmosphere—the mixture of gases that surrounds Earth
fossil fuel—a natural fuel formed from the remains of plants and animals

The area of permanent sea ice is decreasing nearly 10 percent every 10 years.

We need CO_2 in the atmosphere to keep Earth warm enough for us to live. But more CO_2 being released into the atmosphere creates a **greenhouse effect**. As more CO_2 enters the atmosphere, more heat is trapped. Right now there is more CO_2 in the atmosphere than at any point in the last 500,000 years.

Scientists predict that Earth's temperature will likely rise between 3.5° and 6.5°F in the next century. Failing to curb **emissions** within the next 10 years could lead to no summer sea ice in the Arctic by 2040. The winter sea ice would be greatly reduced.

greenhouse effect—the trapping of heat by a thick atmosphere
emission—a substance released into the air

oil drilling in the Arctic

Oil Exploration in the Arctic

The Arctic contains large deposits of oil and natural gas. Companies want to explore the Arctic for these valuable resources. Some of the areas richest in oil are also where polar bears live.

The noisy, rumbling mining process can disturb bears. Oil spills can coat their fur. As bears groom themselves or eat oil-covered seals, they could take in deadly chemicals. Although oil drilling doesn't melt the ice, it does create another challenge in managing the future of polar bears.

The loss of polar bears depends on how fast the sea ice melts. If the ice recedes, there will be fewer seals. Fewer seals mean less food for polar bears. Less food means more polar bears will starve. Scientists predict two-thirds of the world's polar bears will be gone by 2050. Other animals rely on sea ice to live, including seals, walruses, whales, foxes, and even caribou and musk oxen. These animals would be threatened too.

Global warming could put one-fifth to one-third of all Earth's species at risk of extinction by 2100. That's enough to qualify as a mass extinction on the level of the dinosaurs.

Hungry bears will eat garbage and other foods associated with people. This practice is dangerous to both polar bears and people.

As sea ice retreats farther north and is less widespread, seals will become scarce.

People will need to face changes too. Melting glaciers cause the sea levels to rise. People who live near coasts will need to find somewhere new to live. Rainfall patterns will change. People in warmer climates will experience more droughts, and crops will need to be grown in new areas.

The most serious effects of global warming may not be seen for years or decades. But if people do not reduce their greenhouse gas output, effects like the extinction of polar bears will occur. Adults are the ones making the decisions now. But in 20 or 30 years, the world will be in the hands of today's children. If you're a child, this will be your world.

WHAT CAN I DO TO HELP POLAR BEARS?

CHAPTER 4

Solutions

Some polar bears can't swim far enough to find ice.

When faced with a difficult problem like global warming and its effect on polar bears, it can be hard to stay hopeful. But it's not too late. If emissions fall to half their current levels by 2050, people may have a chance to save the sea ice.

The United States is the largest source of pollution that causes global warming.

The first step is to know where the emissions come from. The biggest contributors are the power plants that generate electricity. There are 500,000 of these plants worldwide. Cars, buses, and other forms of transportation also contribute a lot of pollution. In the United States, people have more than 246 million cars. Each car releases CO_2 into the atmosphere.

Some countries are taking steps to reduce emissions. They are promoting wind and solar energy. These processes do not give off CO_2 as they create energy.

Many groups are protesting global warming and raising awareness for polar bears.

Some scientists are working on extreme solutions to global warming. One scientist is researching the use of a giant space umbrella to shield Earth from the sun's rays.

Some propose building a 20,000-foot (6,096 m) hose that would spew sulfur particles into the atmosphere. The sulfur particles would keep sunlight from reaching Earth's surface, and keep the world cooler.

Each of these ideas has its downside. A giant space umbrella would be extremely expensive. Sulfur particles are a form of pollution that causes acid rain. Scientists think of these solutions as last-ditch efforts.

People often wonder about extreme solutions to the polar bears' problem too. Their solutions may seem simple, but they present larger problems.

CAN WE REPLACE ICE WITH LARGE, FLOATING PLATFORMS?

Polar bears hunt mostly through the ice. As the seals come to breathing holes, the bears grab them. Plastic platforms would not act the same way as ice for the seals or polar bears.

WHAT ABOUT MOVING POLAR BEARS TO ANTARCTICA?

Bringing new species into an area is generally not a good idea. There's no guarantee that the bears will be able to hunt the native animals. Or they will be too successful and hunt the animals into extinction.

CAN WE AT LEAST DROP FOOD FOR THEM SO THEY DON'T STARVE?

Polar bears need a lot of food. Their main food source comes from seals—usually seal pups. One polar bear needs to eat more than 40 seals each year. That's a lot of seals! And don't forget that polar bears are hunters. If they began to rely on humans for food, they might forget how to hunt by themselves.

Zoos may someday be the last shelter for polar bears. Polar bears are found in more than 100 zoos today. Survival rates of cubs born in zoos have increased over the years.

But keeping polar bears can be tricky. Not enough space to roam and play often causes pacing and other repetitive behavior in bears. Researchers continue to study ways to reduce polar bears' stress in zoos.

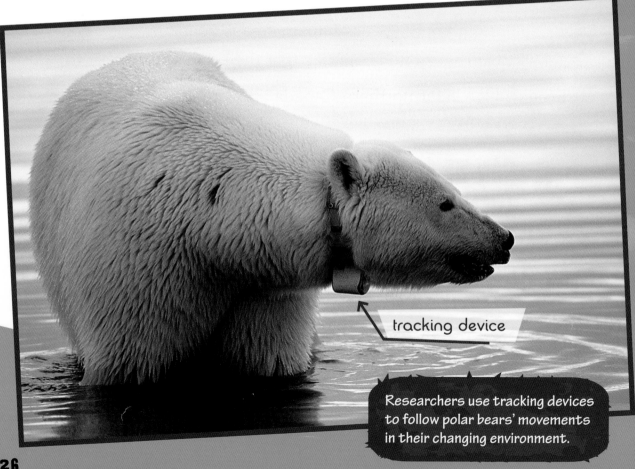

tracking device

Researchers use tracking devices to follow polar bears' movements in their changing environment.

The future of polar bears is still unknown.

Until the end of the century, polar bears are likely to be found in far northern Canada and Greenland, where the last summer sea ice will be available. But the total numbers of polar bears are expected to go down dramatically between now and then.

Scientists will continue to study wild bears. They track bears with satellite collars to see their movements. Scientists may be able to determine the areas where ice will remain the longest. **Sanctuaries** could then be created for the bears. Scientists, and the world, will continue to watch how climate change is affecting the great white polar bears.

sanctuary—a natural area where plants and animals are protected from harm

Reduce Your Carbon Footprint

A carbon footprint is the measure of CO_2 that results from a person's activities for a period of time. The key to lowering your footprint is the word "reduce." These may seem like small steps, but little differences can mean big changes for polar bears.

- Turn off lights when you're not in the room. Even if you'll only be gone five minutes, turn 'em off.

- Unplug electronics when they're not being used. That includes cell phone chargers, TVs, hair dryers, and microwaves. The International Energy Agency estimates that a full 1 percent of the world's CO_2 emissions comes from electronics that are just on stand-by mode.

- Walk, bike, or skateboard rather than getting a car ride for a few blocks to school or a friend's house. Don't forget to get permission from your parents first!

- Do not use drive-throughs at restaurants and do not let your car run when it is not necessary.

- Think about your future. Perhaps you could become a scientist who develops new technology for clean energy. Remember that the next time you're wondering how math and science can help you!

RESOURCES TO HELP POLAR BEARS

NATIONAL WILDLIFE FEDERATION

The National Wildlife Federation is the world's largest conservation organization. The group's goal is to protect wildlife and restore natural habitats. They educate people as a means to protect America's animals.

POLAR BEARS INTERNATIONAL

Polar Bears International is a nonprofit organization dedicated to conservation of the polar bear and its habitat through research and education. The group has gathered information about polar bears that is available to the public.

THE POLAR BEAR SPECIALIST GROUP

The Polar Bear Specialist Group is a professional organization of polar bear biologists. They work to gather scientific knowledge about polar bears and share that information with the public.

WORLD WILDLIFE FUND

As the world's leading conservation organization, the World Wildlife Fund encourages people to take action at every level—local and global Located in 100 countries, the WWF works to educate people about the world around them.

Glossary

atmosphere (AT-muhs-feer)—the mixture of gases that surrounds Earth

emission (ee-MI-shuhn)—a substance released into the air

endangered (in-DAYN-juhrd)—at risk of dying out

Endangered Species Act (in-DAYN-juhrd SPEE-sheez AKT)—a U.S. law designed to protect plant and animal species in danger of dying out

fossil fuel (FAH-suhl FYOOL)—a natural fuel formed from the remains of plants and animals; coal, oil, and natural gas are fossil fuels

global warming (GLOH-buhl WOR-ming)—the gradual temperature rise of Earth's atmosphere

greenhouse effect (GREEN-houss uh-FEKT)—the trapping of heat by a thick atmosphere

sanctuary (SANGK-choo-er-ee)—a natural area where plants and animals are protected from harm

starvation (star-VAY-shuhn)—suffering or dying from lack of food

Read More

Hirsch, Rebecca E. *Top 50 Reasons to Care about Polar Bears: Animals in Peril.* Top 50 Reasons to Care about Endangered Animals. Berkeley Heights, N.J.: Enslow, 2010.

Thomas, Keltie. *Bear Rescue: Changing the Future for Endangered Wildlife.* Firefly Animal Rescue. Buffalo, N.Y.: Firefly Books, 2006.

Wilsdon, Christina. *Polar Bears.* Amazing Animals. Pleasantville, N.Y.: Gareth Stevens Publishing, 2009.

Internet Sites

FactHound offers a safe, fun way to find Internet sites related to this book. All of the sites on FactHound have been researched by our staff.

Here's all you do:

Visit *www.facthound.com*

FactHound will fetch the best sites for you!

Index

Alaska, 5
Arctic, 8, 10, 11, 12, 14, 15, 16, 18, 19
atmosphere, 17, 18, 23, 24

brown bears, 14, 15

Canada, 5, 27
carbon dioxide (CO_2), 17, 18, 22, 23
climate change, 12, 13, 16, 18, 20, 27

emissions, 18, 22, 23
Endangered Species Act, 4
extinction, 4, 20, 25

fossil fuels, 17, 19

global warming, 12, 13, 16, 17, 20, 21,
    22, 23, 24
greenhouse effect, 18
Greenland, 27

hunting, 6, 7, 8, 11, 14, 15, 25

polar bears
    adaptations, 10, 15
    cubs, 4, 6, 7, 26
    food, 6, 7, 8, 9, 14, 20, 25
    in the media, 4, 11
    and people, 7, 20
    populations, 5, 6, 7, 27
    range, 5, 11, 12–13, 19, 27
    size, 6, 7, 9, 14
    starvation, 6, 7, 8, 20
    swimming, 11
pollution, 19, 23, 24
power plants, 17, 23
prey, 8, 9, 14, 15, 20, 25

sanctuaries, 27
sea ice, 8, 9, 11, 12, 13, 15, 18,
    20, 22, 25, 27
seals, 8, 9, 15, 19, 20, 25
solutions, 24–25

zoos, 26